JAMES AND THE GIANT PEACH

by
Roald Dahl

Teacher Guide

Written by
Jean Jamieson

Note

The text used to prepare this guide was the Puffin Books softcover, ©1961 by Roald Dahl. If other editions are used, page references may vary slightly.

Please note: Please assess the appropriateness of this book for the age level and maturity of your students prior to reading and discussing it with your class.

ISBN 1-56137-055-X

To order, contact your local school
supply store, or—

**PAPERBACKS - BMI BOUND BOOKS
TEACHER'S GUIDES - AUDIO-VISUALS
PO BOX 800 - DAYTON, N.J. 08810-0800
Toll Free Phone 1-800-222-8100
*America's Finest Educational Book Distributor***

Table of Contents

Summary 3

About the Author 3

Bulletin Board Idea 4

Initiating Activities 4

Sixteen Sections 5
    Sections contain: Summary, Vocabulary,
    Vocabulary Activity, Questions for Discussion,
    Post-reading Activities

Conclusion 33

Supplementary Activities 34

Teacher Information 40

Bibliography 42

Skills and Strategies

Thinking
Brainstorming, inferring, visualizing

Vocabulary
Synonym/antonym, word mapping

Literary Elements
Characterization, simile, story elements, alliteration

Comprehension
Predicting, cause and effect, comparison/contrast

Writing
Poetry, creative, description

Listening/Speaking
Discussion, drama

Plot Summary

Orphaned at the age of four, James Henry Trotter is sent to live with two selfish, cruel aunts. The story actually begins when James is seven. Given a bag of magic green crystals by an old man, James is promised a better life if he dissolves the crystals in water and drinks the liquid. Unfortunately, James drops the bag in the garden, and the crystals quickly go underground beneath an old peach tree. It is then that the old tree produces a peach that grows to the size of a small house. Discovering a hole in the peach, James crawls inside and finds some creatures waiting for him in a room in the stone of the peach. Detaching the stem of the peach from the tree, the creatures and James start out on a fantastic journey that eventually takes them across the Atlantic Ocean.

(Some suggested topics of interest: Roald Dahl, fantasy, weather, insects and spiders, travel)

About the Author

Roald Dahl was born September 13, 1916, in Llandaff, South Wales. He died November 23, 1990. Dahl was a graduate of the British Public Schools, 1932. He was a fighter pilot in the Royal Air Force from 1939 until 1945. He married actress Patricia Neal in 1953. They were divorced in 1983, and Dahl married Felicity Ann Crosland. Dahl and Neal had five children, Olivia, Tessa, Theo, Ophelia, and Lucy.

Best known as the author of children's books, Dahl was also noted for his short stories for adults, and his enchanting autobiographical descriptions of growing up in England and flying in World War II. His children's fiction is known for its sudden turn into the fantastic and harsh treatment of any adults foolish enough to cause trouble for the young heroes and heroines.

Dahl began by making up stories for his own children, and these became the basis for his career as a children's writer. He felt that the story must move along quickly in order to keep the interest of children, and that an author should know what children like. He once said, "The writer for children should be unconventional and inventive." With that statement, he summarized his own work.

Note: It is not intended that everything presented in this guide be done. Please be selective, and use discretion when choosing the activities you will do with the unit. The choices made should be appropriate for your use and your group of students. A wide range of activities has been provided so that individuals as well as groups may benefit.

Bulletin Board Idea

Cover the bulletin board with plain background paper. Divide the space into three sections. Make a picture of a large peach speared on a spike that is actually a TV antenna atop a large building. Place the picture in the center section of the board.

As the unit progresses, ask student volunteers to write brief summaries of books that are fantasies and to place the summaries on the bulletin board. Place all of those authored by Roald Dahl in one section of the board.

Type of Book: Fantasy

Roald Dahl   Other Authors

Initiating Activities

Make some banners to place in the room to encourage the creative use of imagination. For example: Be Inventive! Originality Counts! You Are Talented! Clever!

Look at the picture in the center of the bulletin board. How do you imagine the peach got on top of the building? (You may want to make an audio tape of student responses.)

Prereading Activity
What do you think of when you see/hear the word FANTASY? (Record student responses.)

Prereading Discussion
What kind of story do you think this will be? On what do you base your opinion? What books have you read which fit into the category of FANTASY? List. What do you like/dislike about FANTASY? Discuss.

Previewing the Book
Look at the cover of the book. What does the illustrator, Chris Van Allsburg, tell about the story? What is floating in the water? What is unusual about the peach? What is the title of the book? Where do you imagine the body of water is located? What do you think the boy might be looking at? Some things to consider: Do you think the boy is all alone? Why is the peach floating on the water? How do you suppose the peach got there? What do you think might happen to the boy and the peach? Make some predictions.

Recommended Procedure
Because of the differing lengths of the chapters of the book, some chapters have been combined and the guide refers to sections rather than chapters. It is up to the teacher as to whether or not to follow the suggested sectioning.

Assessment of the understanding of the vocabulary words by the students may be done by introducing the vocabulary words with each section. The students, either individually or as a group, may then be asked to try to define each word. After the section is read, the vocabulary words may be reviewed and any changes necessary in students' definitions may be made to have them coincide with the context of the section. A dictionary may be used for clarification when needed.

Section 1
Chapter 1, pages 1 through 3

James Henry Trotter is orphaned when he is four years old. Sent to live with two selfish maiden aunts, Aunt Sponge and Aunt Spiker, James leads a very unhappy life.

Vocabulary
paddle p. 1   ramshackle p. 2   desolate p. 3

Vocabulary Activity
Use each of the vocabulary words in a sentence.

Questions for Discussion
1. What kind of life does James Henry Trotter have up until the time he is four years old? (p. 1—James has a happy, "perfect life for a small boy.") Describe his life. (p. 1—James lives peacefully with his mother and father in a beautiful house beside the sea; he has plenty of friends and toys, a sandy beach to run on and an ocean to paddle in.) Would you agree that James has a perfect life for a small boy? Why or why not? Discuss. What would you change about his life at that time—or add to it? Why?

2. What happens to cause James to be alone and frightened in an unfriendly world? (pp. 1 & 2—While in London, Mr. and Mrs. Trotter are eaten by an escaped zoo rhinoceros. Their home must be sold right away.) Where does James go? (p. 2—James is sent to the south of England to live with his two aunts, Aunt Sponge and Aunt Spiker.) How is James treated by the aunts? (pp. 2 & 3—James is...beaten by the aunts for no reason at all...given a bare room resembling a cell...never called by his real name...not allowed to leave the top of the hill...called "you disgusting little beast"...not allowed to have a pet...called "you filthy nuisance"...not allowed to have books or toys...called "you miserable creature"...not allowed to have friends.) How do you think a four-year-old boy should be treated? Discuss.

Post-reading Activities
1. Start a **character attribute web** for James. Add to it as the story continues. (Characterization is the way an author lets the reader know what the characters are like. In **direct characterization**, the author describes the character directly [blue eyes, brown hair, etc.] In **indirect characterization**, the author provides clues about the character through thoughts, speech and actions.)
2. Share something of yours with James. What game, toy or sports equipment would you give to seven-year-old James (his age at the time this story takes place)? Why do you think James will enjoy your gift? **Write a short story** in which you give the gift to James, and tell him why you made this particular choice. Illustrate your story.
3. A **simile** suggests a similarity between two things which are not alike. Intermediary words, such as *like, as, than, similar to, resembles,* etc., are used to highlight the comparison being made.
    The author ends Chapter 1 with the use of a simile. Read the last sentence of this chapter on page 3. What are the things being compared in this sentence? How are they alike? Write your own simile. What two things are being compared in your simile? How are they alike?
4. Start character **attribute webs** for Aunt Spiker and Aunt Sponge. Add to the webs as the story progresses.
5. Will James find a friend? Will the aunts be kinder to James? What do you think might happen next? **Make a prediction.**

Section 2
Chapter 2 through Chapter 4, pages 3 through 11

The adventures of this story take place when James is seven years old. One hot summer day, after working in the garden, James is given a bag of green crystals by an old man. The man tells James to dissolve the crystals in a jug of water, and to drink it all down. The crystals, he says, are magic, and James' life will be changed forever after he drinks them.

Vocabulary

peculiar p. 4	fantastically p. 4	spectacles p. 5
beckoning p. 8	luminous p. 8	furiously p. 10

Vocabulary Activity
Design some marvelous, magic, fantastically luminous SPECTACLES for James. Make an illustration of the spectacles and explain what will happen when James wears them.

Questions for Discussion
1. What are Aunt Sponge, Aunt Spiker and James doing out in the garden on a hot summer day? (p. 4—The aunts are sitting in deck-chairs in the garden, drinking lemonade and watching James chop wood for the kitchen stove.) How do you think James is feeling about his situation as he chops wood? (Opinion—answers will vary. Discuss student opinions.)
2. James annoys the aunts by crying. Aunt Spiker sends James out of her sight. Where does he go? (p. 7—James hides himself behind the clump of laurel bushes.) What does James see emerging from the bushes? (p. 8—James sees a very small old man.) What does the man give to James? (pp. 8 & 9—The man gives James a bag of magic green crystals.) What about you? Do you think you would take such a bag of crystals from a strange man? Why or why not? Explain your answer. What will happen if the crystals escape from the bag? (p. 11—Whoever the crystals meet first will have the full power of their magic.) Do you think James will receive the magic of the crystals, or will they escape? What is your prediction?

Post-reading Activities

1. Start a **story map**. (Although you may start with the information you now have as to the setting, the main character and the problem, things may change as the story continues. The story map may also be changed to reflect this.)
2. The author uses poetry to have the two aunts describe themselves, and to banter back and forth (pages 5 & 6). Make an **illustration** of a comic character. Write a **humorous poem** to describe the character.
3. As James chops the wood, he thinks about what other children in the world are doing at the same moment (page 6). If you were chopping wood instead of James, and were granted one wish, what would that wish be? Why would you make that particular wish? **Write down your wish** and the **reasons** for making it.
4. What will James do with the green crystals? **Make a prediction.**

Section 3
Chapter 5 through Chapter 7, pages 11 through 20

James runs toward the kitchen. Trying to avoid the aunts on his way, James twists a foot and drops the bag. The green crystals escape from the bag and all of them go into the ground around the old peach tree. A peach starts to grow on the tree and it gets larger and larger.

Vocabulary

centipedes p. 12	hideous p. 13	gracious p. 14
ridiculous p. 16	absolutely p. 16	extraordinary p. 16
mammoth p. 17	inspecting p. 19	cautiously p. 19
massive p. 19		

Vocabulary Activity

List a synonym and an antonym and make word maps for the vocabulary words: HIDEOUS, RIDICULOUS, ABSOLUTELY, EXTRAORDINARY, MAMMOTH, CAUTIOUSLY, and MASSIVE. (See the framework on page 9.)

For example:

Vocabulary Word	One Synonym	One Antonym
hideous	repulsive	attractive
ridiculous	ludicrous	sensible
absolutely	perfectly	imperfectly
extraordinary	unusual	ordinary
mammoth	huge	tiny
cautiously	warily	carelessly
massive	large	slight

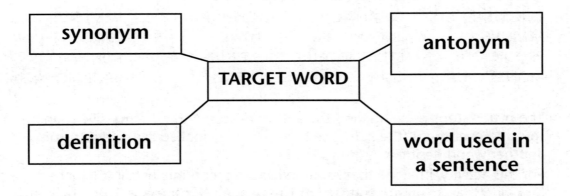

Questions for Discussion

1. What happens as James runs to the house? (p. 11—James swerves to avoid the aunts. In doing so, he slips and falls when he is underneath the old peach tree. James drops the bag and the green crystals escape.) Is James able to recover some of the crystals? (p. 12—No, James is not able to recover any of the crystals. The crystals all burrow into the ground around the tree.) What does James remember about the crystals? (p. 12—James remembers that the crystals will work their magic on "whoever they meet first, be it bug, insect, animal, or tree.") What do you think might happen? (Discuss student responses.)

2. As the aunts watch the peach, James starts to get a special feeling inside. What does he feel? (p. 14—"Something is about to happen. Something peculiar is about to happen.") There are other clues that add to the feeling James has. What are some of them? (p. 14—James could feel it in the air about him. There is a sudden stillness in the garden. There is not a breath of wind and the sun is blazing down on the garden.) Have you ever had a feeling that something was about to happen? (Share and discuss student responses.)

3. What plans do the aunts have for the peach? (pp. 19 & 20—Aunt Sponge wants to get a shovel and start eating the peach. Aunt Spiker wants to figure out some way to make money from the peach.) What do you think you would do with the giant peach? Discuss student suggestions.

Post-reading Activities

1. On page 17, the peach is described as being MAMMOTH. What other words could be used to describe its size? For example:

COLOSSAL	GIGANTIC	HUGE	IMMENSE
MASSIVE	ENORMOUS	TITANIC	GARGANTUAN
PRODIGIOUS	STUPENDOUS	ELEPHANTINE	PONDEROUS
MONSTROUS	GIANT	GREAT	BROBDIGNAGIAN

2. The peach stops growing, and the author relates, "And the massive round fruit towered over them (the aunts) so high that they looked like midgets from another world beside it." (page 19)
    For this activity, imagine that Aunt Spiker is 5 feet 6 inches tall (66 inches). Knowing that, **estimate the size of the peach.** [Hint: (page 19): The peach became "nearly as tall as the tree that it was growing on, as tall and wide, in fact, as a small house."]

3. Imagine a fruit and vegetable town! What might it look like? What unusual things might take place there? **Write a story in prose or poetry form** about a town in which all of the buildings and vehicles are made of fruits and/or vegetables. Make illustrations for your story.

4. Did the green crystals make the peach grow? Will something else happen because of the green crystals? What do you think might happen next? **Make a prediction.**

Section 4
Chapter 8 through Chapter 10, pages 20 through 26

The peach gets as large as a small house. The aunts have a fence built around the peach and charge admission to sightseers. James is locked in his room, and only let out at night so that he can clean up after the crowd. When close to the peach, James sees a hole in it, near the bottom. Crawling into the peach, James discovers a tunnel that leads to a room in the stone. When James enters the room, a voice welcomes him.

Vocabulary

marvel p. 20	shilling p. 20	seething p. 21
miraculous p. 21	murky p. 25	curious p. 25
bittersweet p. 25	uphill p. 25	gigantic p. 25
stone p. 25	bolt p. 25	

Vocabulary Activity

In a tongue twister, use the vocabulary words MARVEL, MIRACULOUS, and MURKY, and other words that begin with the same letter/sound. Try to say the tongue twister three times without making an error. Then try to say it faster and faster. Increase the length of the tongue twister for more of a challenge. For example:

Murky Miraculous Marvels Made Monday Marvelous
Meaningful Murky Miraculous Marvels Made Monday Marvelous
Many Meaningful Murky Miraculous Marvels Made Monday Marvelous

Questions for Discussion

1. What do the aunts do to prepare for the sightseers? (p. 20—The aunts have carpenters build a strong fence around the peach, and they get a large bunch of tickets so they can charge everyone for coming in to see the peach.) What is James allowed to do? (p. 21—Nothing—James is locked in his bedroom, so he will not get in the aunts' way.) Can you think of some additional reasons why the aunts might want to keep James locked in his room? Discuss.

2. Why does James feel a shiver of excitement running over the skin of his back? (pp. 23 & 24—James thinks that something strange is about to happen to him.) What kinds of emotions might cause "shivers"? Discuss and list student responses (for example: excitement, fear, anger).

3. What does James do as he crawls along the tunnel in the peach? (p. 25—James catches some of the dripping juice on his tongue and tastes it. He also takes bites out of the peach as he goes along.) How do you think James looks and feels as he crawls inside the peach? Discuss and list descriptive words. (For example: sticky, soggy, syrupy, tacky, gummy, gluey, gooey, mucilaginous, gelatinous…)

Post-reading Activities

1. Because the aunts live in the south of England, the currency of the United Kingdom is mentioned in the story (page 20). (The following information regarding the value of UK currency is found in several dictionaries.) The aunts charge **one shilling** per person to see the giant peach. Although no longer in use, one shilling had the value of **1/20 of a pound sterling**. One pound sterling had the value of **100 pence**, pence being the plural for penny. How many **pence** would one have to have in order to purchase a ticket to see the peach? (five) How much would it cost your class to see the peach?

2. List as many things as you can think of that are **peach-flavored** or made with peaches. **For example:**

peach pie	peach ice cream
peach cobbler	peach yogurt
peach jam	peach flavored hard candy
peach jelly	peach gelatin
peach preserves	

    Which of the peach things on your list would you like to try? Why?

3. In three minutes, how many words can you list that **rhyme** with PEACH? **For example:** *beach, bleach, leech, reach, teach, each, beech, leach, speech, impeach, outreach, beseech, overreach...*

4. A **limerick** is a poem consisting of five lines. The first, second, and fifth lines rhyme, as do the third and fourth. The fifth line often takes a humorous twist. Write a limerick about the peach.

James tunnels away inside the peach
Eating bits of wall within his reach.
He sinks now and then,
But comes back up once again.
New methods of locomotion he now can teach.

5. Where is the door? Who is speaking to James? What do you think might happen next? **Make a prediction.**

Section 5
Chapter 11 through Chapter 13, pages 26 through 35

James meets the large creatures that have been waiting for him. There are insects and a spider about the same size as James. Each has eaten at least one green crystal as it passed through the soil. The spider makes beds for all and they settle in for a good night's sleep.

Vocabulary

reclining p. 26	intently p. 26	scarlet p. 26
magnificent p. 26	famished p. 27	delicately p. 27
positively p. 27	disagreeable p. 28	marvelous p. 29
slither p. 29	approval p. 29	withering p. 29
scornful p. 29	colossal p. 30	hysterics p. 31
gossamer p. 31	complicated p. 33	ambled p. 33
literally p. 34	wretched p. 34	

Vocabulary Activity

Use the vocabulary word (or words), that make(s) the most sense to complete each sentence.

1. The girl _____ over to the chair and sat down. (ambled)
2. The boy wore a _____-colored tie to match his red socks. (scarlet)
3. He was so_____ when he got home from school, he ate some dry bread. (famished)

13

4. She is mad because the lock on her locker has a _____ combination. (complicated)

5. He has a _____ chair that is absolutely m_____ and m_____. (reclining, magnificent, marvelous)

Questions for Discussion

1. After James enters the room in the stone of the peach, what do the creatures talk about among themselves? (p. 27—The creatures talk about their hunger.) What is the reaction of James to this talk? (p. 27—James is terrified.) What do you imagine James is thinking as the creatures speak of their hunger, and why would he think that? (Opinion—answers will vary.)

2. What do the creatures tell James about their hunger? (p. 28—They tell James not to be frightened. They will not hurt him.) Do you think the creatures would act differently toward James if he was not considered to be "one of the crew"? (p. 28) Discuss.

3. On page 28, the Old-Green-Grasshopper says to James, "We've been waiting for you all day long." How do you think the creatures knew James would be coming? Discuss student responses.

4. As James drifts off to sleep, how is he feeling about his new friends? (p. 35—James is beginning to like his new friends very much. They seem kind and helpful to him, and he is comfortable with them.) Has James thought about his aunts and his absence from their home since entering the peach? Do you think James' absence has been noticed by the aunts? Discuss.

Post-reading Activities

1. The Centipede is wearing boots. (p. 28)
Design a new pair of boots for him or something else for him to wear in their place. (You might want to think of something that will make it easy for the Centipede to put on and remove what you design.) **Explain** how your designed footwear differs from the boots the Centipede wears.

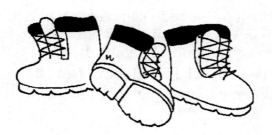

2. The Centipede seems proud to refer to himself as a pest (page 29). Print the word CENTIPEDE vertically on a separate sheet of paper. Use each letter of the word CENTIPEDE as the first letter of a **descriptive word** that you think goes with the story character.

For example:
> Cranky
> Explosive
> Nagging
> Testy
> Irritating
> Petulant
> Exasperating
> Demanding
> Egocentric

3. Are the aunts looking for James? What will happen in the morning? What do you think might happen next? **Make a prediction.**

Section 6
Chapter 14 through Chapter 15, pages 35 through 40

In the morning, the Centipede uses his sharp jaws to nibble through the stem that holds the peach to the tree. The peach rolls down the steep hill, crushing everything in its way, which includes the aunts. Although they do not know their destination, the creatures feel that anything will be better than what they are leaving behind.

Vocabulary

heave p. 35	obviously p. 36	depart p. 36
ghastly p. 36	repulsive p. 36	lurch p. 36
venomous p. 37	insidiously p. 38	visible p. 39
horrid p. 39	gaped p. 39	panicked p. 39
jostling p. 40		

Vocabulary Activity

Put the vocabulary words in alphabetical order. Number the words. Define all of the odd-numbered words.

depart

gaped

ghastly

heave

horrid
insidiously
jostling
lurch
obviously
panicked
repulsive
venomous
visible

Questions for Discussion

1. There is a great hubbub when James awakens in the morning. What is happening? (p. 36—The creatures are getting ready to depart.) How is the peach being detached from the tree? (p. 36—The Centipede is nibbling at the stem with his very sharp jaws.) Do the creatures know or care where they are going in the peach? What do you think may be the reason(s) for their attitude? Discuss.

2. Why are the aunts unable to get out of the way of the careening peach? (pp. 39 & 40—The aunts panicked and got in one another's way, preventing escape.) Do you imagine that anyone is sorry that the aunts got rolled over by the peach? (Opinion—answers will vary.) Discuss.

Post-reading Activities

1. Add to the Centipede's **rhyme**, page 37. Describe a creature that the friends might see on the journey in the peach.

2. What **inscriptions** might be placed on the tombstones of the aunts? Imagine that it is up to you to make that decision.
(See examples, next page.)

Aunt Sponge
Here lies Aunt Sponge,
Once squishy and white.
She was run over by a peach
Without getting a bite.

Aunt Spiker
Here lies Aunt Spiker,
Once skinny, loud and mean.
She is now quiet and subdued,
With barely enough left to be seen.

3. Where will the peach land? Will the creatures be safe in the peach? What do you think might happen next? **Make a prediction.**

Section 7
Chapter 16 through Chapter 17, pages 40 through 47

As the peach rolls down the steep hill, the adventurers are flung about inside the peach and are badly battered and bruised. The peach reaches the cliffs along the English shoreline and is flung out onto the ocean, where it floats on the surface. The adventurers climb to the top of the peach to take a look at the peach's landing site.

Vocabulary

hurtling p. 40	paddock p. 41	stampeding p. 41
tremendous p. 41	destruction p. 42	hayrides p. 42
serenely p. 43	indestructible p. 43	chaos p. 43
unfortunate p. 44	disentangle p. 45	trifle p. 46
chorused p. 46	vertically p. 47	

Vocabulary Activity
Put the vocabulary words into sets of two. Since there are fourteen vocabulary words, there will be seven sets of two words each. Use each set of words in a sentence. Illustrate one sentence.

Questions for Discussion
1. What kind of journey do the occupants of the peach have while it rolls down the hill? (p. 44—"No travelers had ever had a more terrible journey than these unfortunate creatures.") Could anything have been done before the descent that might have helped the occupants of the peach? Discuss.

2. Which of the creatures is optimistic and which creature is pessimistic about the landing site of the peach? (p. 45—The Old-Green-Grasshopper is optimistic, betting that the place where the peach landed is "somewhere good." The Earthworm is pessimistic, telling everyone, "We are probably at the bottom of a coal mine.") If you were one of the peach travelers, do you think your attitude would be more like that of the Grasshopper or the Earthworm? Why? Discuss student responses.

3. What do the travelers do after the peach lands? (p. 46—They decide to take a look around from the top of the peach.) Why do they decide to look from the top of the peach rather than the side? (p. 46—The Grasshopper advised them not to go out of the side entrance when they didn't know where they were.) What do you think of the Grasshopper's advice? (Opinion—answers will vary. Discuss student opinions.)

Post-reading Activities

1. **Cause and Effect: Cause**: a reason something happens (answers the question **why**). **Effect**: result of a cause (answers the question **what**).

    Start with the Centipede nibbling through the stem of the peach. What **effect** does this have on the peach and the adventurers inside? (Mark the causes with "C" and the effects with "E.")

    For example: In order to free the peach from the tree, the Centipede nibbles through the stem of the peach [C] and the peach rolls down the hill. [E] (One cause may have several effects.)

    A. The peach rolls down the hill and rolls over the aunts on the way, killing them.
    B. The peach continues to roll down the hill and the adventurers inside get tossed about and injured.
    C. The peach continues to roll down the hill and is flung off the shore cliffs onto the ocean.

    Use a different set of circumstances to illustrate a cause and effect situation.

2. Start **attribute webs** for each of the creatures in the peach.
3. Do some research. Find out about the famous cliffs along the English coast (White Cliffs of Dover).
4. What will come into view from the top of the peach? Will the travelers be happy?

    What do you think might happen next? **Make a prediction.**

Section 8
Chapter 18, pages 47 through 54

The travelers discover they have landed on water. The quick current has already carried the peach away from the shore and there is no land in sight. The Earthworm declares they will perish, but James assures the travelers that the peach is floating nicely. The Earthworm then declares they will starve, and once again James is reassuring, telling the travelers they can survive by eating the peach. Everything seems to be fine as the peach sails on the sea.

Vocabulary

current p. 47	vast p. 47	bibbling p. 47
disappointment p. 48	perish p. 48	grisly p. 49
starvation p. 49	affectionately p. 50	glorious p. 51
bluebottle p. 52		

Vocabulary Activity
Do the **Vocabulary Word Search Puzzle #1** found in the **Supplementary Activities** section of this guide.

Questions for Discussion
1. What is the first problem the Earthworm points out to the travelers? (p. 48— The Earthworm says they will perish in the water.) How does James calm his friends? (p. 48—James tells them the peach is floating beautifully.) Why do you think the peach is floating so nicely? (Opinion—answers will vary. Discuss.) Ask for volunteers to prepare experiments for ideas offered during the discussion.
2. What is the second problem pointed out by the Earthworm? (p. 49—The Earthworm says they will starve.) How does James solve this problem? (p. 50—James reminds all they have the peach to eat.) Are there any possible food alternatives for the travelers? Discuss.

Post-reading Activities
1. The Centipede sings about some of the strange and succulent things he has eaten (pages 52–54). The four lines of each verse rhyme. Add a **verse** to the Centipede's song, or create your own poem about some things you like to eat.

For example:

Oh, many strange and glorious things have gone into my belly.
Like sandwiches of peanut butter and roast beef—never mind the jelly,
And fizzy sodas of chocolate ice cream and lemon while watching the telly.
Oh, the best concoctions I've ever had did not come from an ordinary deli.

2. Make a class **recipe book** of extraordinary concoctions. Illustrate each contribution.

3. Make an **illustration** of one dish mentioned by the Centipede in his song that you think to be especially humorous.

4. Will the peach continue to float? Will the travelers be rescued? What do you think might happen next? **Make a prediction.**

Section 9
Chapter 19 through Chapter 20, pages 54 through 61

Sharks spot the peach and come to devour it. The travelers look to James to solve the problem, and he devises a plan. Using the Earthworm as bait to attract the seagulls flying overhead, and string spun by the silkworm and spider, James will tie seagulls to the stem of the peach. With enough gulls attached, the peach will be lifted out of the water.

Vocabulary

anxiously p. 55	cruising p. 55	perambulator p. 56
lunge p. 56	aghast p. 56	froth p. 56
pandemonium p. 56	pathetically p. 56	

Vocabulary Activity
Do the **Vocabulary Crossword Puzzle #1** found in the **Supplementary Activities** section of this guide.

Questions for Discussion

1. What do the travelers see in the water? (p. 55—They see sharks in the water.) Is this a cause for concern? (p. 56—Yes. The sharks furiously attack the peach.) To whom do the creatures turn for help? (p. 56—The creatures ask James to solve the problem.) Why do you think the creatures depend on James to solve the problems? (Opinion—answers will vary. Discuss.)

2. What solution does James offer? What creatures must play major roles in the solution? (pp. 57–60—The Silkworm and Spider are to spin "string" for James to use to tie seagulls to the stem of the peach. The Earthworm is to act as bait, to attract seagulls near enough to the peach for James to loop string around the neck of each one. When enough seagulls have been harnessed and tied to the peach, the peach will be lifted out of the water.) Does this sound like a workable plan to you? Do you have any suggestions or alternatives to offer? Discuss.

Post-reading Activities

1. When hearing of James' plan to elevate the peach, the creatures shout out their opinions (page 59). What words having the **same or similar meaning** as those on page 59 could be added ? Make a list. **For example:**

ludicrous	asinine	outrageous	unbelievable
laughable	crazy	outlandish	rubbish
foolish	preposterous	incredible	nonsense
twaddle	drivel	bosh	bunk
baloney	hooey	garbage	piffle

   Which word from your list would you choose to use? Why?

2. Imagine that you are an investigative reporter. You are in a helicopter above the peach, viewing the shark attack. You are unable to take along cameras of any kind; there is no visual media showing the attack. Your listeners are anxiously awaiting the description of the scene. Your air time is limited. What will you say? How will you say it?

   Write your **commentary,** and practice your delivery. With a partner, listen to one another's descriptions of the scene.

3. Will the Spider and the Silkworm spin enough "string"? Will the plan work? What do you think might happen next? **Make a prediction.**

Section 10
Chapter 21 through Chapter 23, pages 61 through 70

With the harnessing of five hundred and two seagulls, the peach is lifted out of the water and up into the sky. The travelers go out on the top of the peach to celebrate. While there, they notice a ship below. Unfortunately, the officers of the ship believe the peach to be a secret weapon. When the captain describes what he sees through his telescope, the other officers question his sobriety. While this is happening on the ship, the peach disappears into a cloud.

Prediction: *Predict the number of seagulls to be harnessed to the peach in order for the plan to be successful.*

Vocabulary

boiling p. 61	exhorting p. 62	frantically p. 62
tethered p. 64	hovered p. 65	delicately p. 65
majestically p. 66	ascent p. 67	clambered p. 68
funnels p. 69	teeming p. 69	

Vocabulary Activity

Do the **Vocabulary Review #1**—"Synonym or Antonym?"—found in the **Supplementary Activities** section of this guide.

Questions for Discussion

1. Is James able to harness seagulls in the manner planned? (p. 64—Yes. With all of the travelers working together, James is able to harness the seagulls.) How many seagulls have to be harnessed for the peach to be lifted out of the water? (p. 66—It takes five hundred and two seagulls to lift the peach out of the water and up into the sky.) Compare the predicted numbers to the 502 seagulls mentioned in the book. Discuss reasons for discrepancies.

2. Which of the travelers is able to asses the damage done to the peach by the sharks? (p. 67—Miss Spider inspects the bottom of the peach.) What does Miss Spider report to the others? (p. 68—Miss Spider reports that there is only minor damage to the peach.) Do you agree or disagree with the author's explanation of the sharks inability to eat the peach that follows Miss Spider's report? Why? What alternative reason(s) could be given for only minor damage to the peach?

Post-reading Activities

1. You are in charge of the communications room of the ship the *Queen Mary.* The captain has ordered you to send a message to the Queen of England. You are to tell the Queen that an object believed to be a secret weapon has been sighted. Devise a **coded message** to send to the Queen.

2. A **chant** is a rhythmic little verse that helps to keep a meter. Write an original chant for the Centipede to say to the Silkworm and Miss Spider to encourage them to spin more and more silk string for harnessing the seagulls (p. 6). **For example:**

   Come now, Silkworm! Come now, Spider!
   Spin that string. Get it thicker and wider!
   Cover all the furniture. Cover the entire floor.
   We just don't have enough. Spin us more and more.

3. The travelers express their joy at the ascent of the peach in different ways (pp. 66 & 67). Create something that you think **illustrates the joy** felt by one of the travelers. It may be in the form of visual art, prose, poetry, music, dance, or any combination of these forms.

4. Where will the seagulls take the peach? Will the travelers be safe now? What do you think might happen next? **Make a prediction.**

Section 11
Chapter 24 through Chapter 25, pages 70 through 79

The travelers continue their celebrating. Old-Green-Grasshopper plays music for the rest, and keeps them all spellbound. James learns more about his new friends, and the Centipede sings for the group.

Vocabulary

spellbound p. 71	inferior p. 72	fascinating p. 72
katydids p. 73	rambunctious p. 74	vital p. 75
modestly p. 75	saucy p. 76	

Vocabulary Activity

In three minutes, how many words can you make from the letters of the word **RAMBUNCTIOUS**? (Here are some: *ram, tam, ton, son, no, so, to, mob, sob, cub, cut, cur, sir, stir, bun, nab, tab, stab, cab, crab, tram, am, cot, rot, not, rust, bust, must, cram, stun, most, coast, boast, oat, coat, moat, tub, rub, rat, bat, mat, at, cat...*)

Questions for Discussion

1. How do the travelers continue to celebrate the ascent of the peach? (p. 71—The Old-Green-Grasshopper plays music for the other members of the group.) How is it possible for the Grasshopper to play music? (p. 71—The music is much like that of a violin. The Grasshopper uses the thigh of his back leg like a bow on the edge of his wing.) What piece of music would you like the Grasshopper to play for you? Why? Discuss music preferences.

2. Why does Miss Spider think spiders are treated unfairly? (p. 76—Miss Spider feels that she is not loved, yet she does nothing but good by catching mosquitoes and flies in her web.) What happened to Miss Spider's father? (p. 76—Aunt Sponge flushed Miss Spider's father down the plug hole in the bathtub. His family never saw him again.) Do you like spiders? Why do you think it is that most people do not like spiders? (Opinion—answers will vary. Discuss opinions expressed by students.)

Post-reading Activities

1. Choose one of the "creature" travelers to **investigate**. Report your findings, emphasizing the positive and unusual information about the creature. (Earthworm, Silkworm, Glowworm, Centipede, Spider, Ladybug, Grasshopper)

2. The songs of the Centipede use the **limerick** poetry form. A limerick is a poem of five lines. The first, second, and fifth lines rhyme, as do the third and fourth. The fifth line often takes a humorous twist.

    Write an original limerick, using one of the characters in the story as the subject of your limerick. **For example:**

    > *There once was a Centipede, a pest,*
    > *Who put everyone's patience to the test.*
    > *He was bossy and loud,*
    > *With his head in a cloud,*
    > *But could sing songs that were the best.*

3. Is the Centipede all right? Is something wrong with the peach? What do you think might happen next? **Make a prediction.**

Section 12
Chapter 26 through Chapter 27, pages 79 through 88

As the Centipede dances wildly, he falls off the peach. James asks the Silkworm to spin once again, and he grabs the silk string. Telling the others to hold onto the Silkworm, James ties the end of the string around his waist and goes after the Centipede. James rescues the Centipede and brings him back to the top of the peach. The travelers decide to stay on top for the night, and see Cloud-Men making hailstones. The Centipede angers the Cloud-Men and the travelers have the hailstones thrown their way. Retreating to the inside of the peach, the travelers wait for the attack to end.

Vocabulary

teetering p. 79	frantically p. 79	companions p.81
menacing p. 81	overwhelming p. 81	lurking p. 82
stealthy p. 82	wraithlike p. 82	imbeciles p. 85
loathsome p. 86	evidently p. 87	infuriated p. 87

Vocabulary Activity
Match the synonym to the vocabulary word.

Synonym	Vocabulary Word	
repulsive	_____	(loathsome)
agitatedly	_____	(frantically)
overpowering	_____	(overwhelming)
angered	_____	(infuriated)
threatening	_____	(menacing)

Questions for Discussion

1. How does James plan to rescue the Centipede? (pp. 79 & 80—James has the Silkworm spin silk string. He ties the loose end around his waist, and tells the others to hold on to the Silkworm. If they feel three tugs, they are all to pull up the string. James goes over the side of the peach in search of the Centipede.) Is James successful? (p. 80—Yes. James swims around in the ocean until he finds the Centipede.) Do you think James is a hero? Why? Why not? Discuss.

2. Where do the travelers decide to spend the night? (p. 81—They decide to stay on the top of the peach for the night.) Why do they make this decision? (p. 81—The Grasshopper advises the others, telling them it will be safer to be on the top of the peach. If anything should happen, they will be ready for it.) Do you agree or disagree with the advice of the Grasshopper? Why? Discuss.

3. What angers the Cloud-Men? What do they do? (pp. 85-87—The taunting of the Centipede angers the Cloud-Men. They throw hailstones at the travelers and the peach.) How do the travelers get some protection? (p. 88—The travelers finally go inside the peach.) Why do you think the Centipede continued to taunt the Cloud-Men after the others pleaded with him to be quiet? Discuss.

Post-reading Activities

1. On page 82, the author does some comparing between traveling by airplane and traveling by peach. Continue the **comparison** on a T-Diagram.

TRAVEL BY PEACH	TRAVEL BY AIRPLANE
quiet	noisy
slow	fast
powered by seagulls	powered by engines

2. Make an **illustration** of a Cloud-Man. Give your Cloud-Man a name, and tell something about him.
3. Have the travelers seen the last of the Cloud-Men? Will the seagulls tire of their load? What do you think might happen next? **Make a prediction.**

Section 13
Chapter 28 through Chapter 30, pages 89 through 99

While the travelers are inspecting the damaged peach, they notice a large arch in the clouds. The Cloud-Men are painting a rainbow. Unfortunately, the path of the peach causes it to bump into the middle of the rainbow, breaking it into two pieces. One Cloud-Man tries to reach the peach by way of one of the silk strings. The Centipede snaps that string from the stem, and the seagull takes the Cloud-Man away. This action infuriates the other Cloud-Men, and they start throwing things at the peach. The Centipede gets covered with thick purple paint that dries quickly, encasing and immobilizing him. A black cloud sends down a wall of water that frightens the travelers but cleans off the Centipede.

Vocabulary

arch p. 89

malevolently p. 92

encased p. 95

considered p. 96

deluge p. 98

hypnotized p. 90

kipper p. 93

detest p. 95

proposal p. 96

enthralled p. 91

flabbergasted p. 93

permanently p. 95

immense p. 97

Vocabulary Activity

Match the definition to the vocabulary word.

<u>Definition</u>	<u>Vocabulary Word</u>
loathe	_____(detest)
beguiled	_____(enthralled)
downpour	_____(deluge)
astonished	_____(flabbergasted)
meanly	_____(malevolently)
huge	_____(immense)

Questions for Discussion

1. What are the Cloud-Men doing when seen again by the travelers? (p. 91—The Cloud-Men are painting a rainbow.) What causes a problem this time? (p. 92—The peach bumps into the rainbow, causing it to break into two pieces.) The Cloud-Man angered by this accident climbs down the silk string toward the peach, but never reaches the peach itself. What do you think he might have done to the travelers and to the peach had he reached his destination? (Opinion—answers will vary. Discuss.)

2. Why does the Centipede get covered with purple paint? (p. 94—The Cloud-Men are angry and start throwing everything they can put their hands on. One Cloud-Man dumps a can of purple paint on the Centipede.) What happens to the Centipede? (pp. 94 & 95—The paint dries and hardens, which encases and immobilizes the Centipede. How is the problem solved? (pp. 97 & 98—An immense black cloud dumps a wall of water onto the peach. This washes the paint off of the Centipede.) Do you think water without such force would have worked just as well to remove the paint? Why or why not? Discuss.

Post-reading Activities

1. Make **illustrations** to go with some of the Cloud-Men incidents described in the book. Make captions for the illustrations, to identify the incidents. Try to think of some ways to give the illustrations three-dimensional effects.*

OR

   Help to make a large **class mural** depicting the sky with large Cloud-Men busy at work. Use materials that will give the mural three-dimensional effects.* (*cotton, lace, netting, thread, colored tissue paper, feathers, glitter, colored glue, etc.)

2. The Centipede is delighted to be free from the paint. Make up a **cheer** for him to say. **For example:**

FREE!

Give me an F

Give me an R

Give me some E-E-Es

I'm as happy as two Bumble Bees.

No more paint on feet and knees.

I'm the dancing Centipede, if you please.

Give me an F

Give me an R

Give me some E-E-Es

I'm the dancing Centipede, if you please.

3. Will the Centipede get into more trouble? Is this the end of the Cloud-Men? What do you think might happen next? **Make a prediction.**

Section 14
Chapter 31 through Chapter 36, pages 99 through 107

The travelers spend the rest of the night on the top of the peach. They see a Cloud-Men's City, and pass by without incident. At daylight, land is sighted by the Centipede. The travelers conclude that it is the City of New York. They have crossed the Atlantic Ocean overnight! Seagulls are freed one at a time, to provide a gentle descent for the peach. All goes well until a commuter plane severs all of the silken strings and the peach plummets to the city below. In the meantime, the city and country are preparing for the worst, thinking the peach is a huge bomb.

Vocabulary

sinister p. 100	toboggans p. 100	melancholy p. 101
horizon p. 101	smithereens p. 103	interrupted p. 103
announcements p. 103	population p. 103	subway p. 103
plummeted p. 106	stupor p. 106	precisely p. 107
pinnacle p. 107		

Vocabulary Activity
Do the **Vocabulary Word Search Puzzle #2** found in the **Supplementary Activities** section of this guide.

Questions for Discussion
1. What do the travelers see at daybreak? (p. 101—The travelers see land with streets and buildings.) Why is the Grasshopper certain that they are not looking at England? (p. 102—The Grasshopper sees buildings taller than those built in England.) What does James think about the scene below? (p. 102—James thinks the tall buildings are skyscrapers in America.) What other identifying characteristics might one look for from an aerial-view perspective? Discuss. (landmarks, rivers, lakes, highways, train tracks, etc.) (See Post-reading Activity #3.)
2. What do the people in the City of New York think about the large object in the sky above them? (p. 103—The people think the peach is an enormous bomb.) Why do you think the people would react in such a manner? (This book has a copyright date of 1961.) Discuss. (See **Supplementary Activities**, p. 34.)

3. How do the travelers plan to land the peach? (p. 102—The plan is to have the Centipede cut seagulls loose one-at-a-time until the peach gently descends to land.) Is the plan a success? (p. 105—The plan progresses successfully until a commuter plane slices through the remaining silken strings, freeing all of the seagulls at once.) Do you think the speed of descent of the peach, fast or slow, might have differing effects on the people in the city? Explain your answer.

Post-reading Activities
1. **Compare** the Cloud-Men **weather-related activities** to the actual causes of the weather conditions. For example:

Cloud-Men Weather Conditions	**Actual Weather Conditions**
Condition: Hailstones	Condition: Hailstones
Cause: Rolled from handfuls of cloud	Cause:
Condition: Rainbow	Condition: Rainbow
Cause: Painted by Cloud-Men	Cause:
Condition: Snow	Condition: Snow
Cause: Snow Machine	Cause:
Condition: Thunder	Condition: Thunder
Cause: Huge Drums	Cause:
Condition: Frost	Condition: Frost
Cause: Frost Factories	Cause:

Choose **one weather condition** to study in depth. Share your findings with the group.

2. Make a **cartoon** that shows the reaction of someone in the City of New York to the peach overhead. Put a **caption** with the cartoon.

3. Use the key on a **world map** to determine the **approximate distance** the group has traveled between the White Cliffs of Dover, England, and the City of New York, USA.

4. On what famous **landmark** does the peach land? (p. 107—Empire State Building) Find out more about this famous building. Where is it? When was it built? How tall is it? What are its distinguishing features? Is it the tallest building in the world today?

5. Have the travelers been injured in the landing? What will happen to the peach? What do you think might happen next? **Make a prediction.**

Section 15
Chapter 37, pages 107 through 115

Viewed from the observation roof, the creatures create fear in the hearts of the grown men of the police force and fire department. However, when James appears and introduces each of the creatures, fear subsides and the welcoming begins.

Vocabulary

binoculars p. 108   observation p. 108   commotion p. 109

Vocabulary Activity

Do the **Vocabulary Crossword Puzzle #2** found in the **Supplementary Activities** section of this guide.

Questions for Discussion

1. What is the initial reaction of the men of the police and fire departments when they see the creatures? (pp. 108–110—Initially, the reaction is that of fear.) Why do you think the men are afraid? Discuss causes of fear.
2. What happens to cause a change of attitude? (pp. 110–115—James appears and introduces each of the creatures.) Why do you think the appearance of James has a calming effect on the men? What do you think would have happened had James not been with the creatures? Discuss.

Post-reading Activities

1. James introduces the creatures in **rhyme** (pages 112–115). Use a rhyming form to introduce a different creature to the crowd, or to introduce yourself.
2. When the chiefs of the police and fire departments are giving possible names to the creatures, pages 109 & 110, are those names real or imaginary? Are the names similar to those a different author of children's books might use (for example, Dr. Seuss)?
    Use your imagination to come up with a **new creature** and a name for it. Make an illustration of your creature and list its essential characteristics.
3. Will the people in the crowd welcome the travelers? Will James find a home? What do you think might happen next? **Make a prediction.**

Section 16
Chapter 38 through Chapter 39, pages 115 through 119

The travelers are welcomed by the Mayor of New York City, and a ticker-tape parade follows. As the peach is transported on a flat bed truck, children climb aboard and eventually devour the peach, leaving only a well-licked stone. The stone becomes a monument, and a home for James, in Central Park. The creatures become rich and successful, and all ends happily for the travelers.

Vocabulary

escorted p. 115	steeplejacks p. 115
ticker-tape parade p. 115	hoisted p. 115

Vocabulary Activity

Do the **Vocabulary Review #2**—"Synonym or Antonym?"— found in the **Supplementary Activities** section of this guide.

Questions for Discussion

1. What becomes of the travelers in their new country? (pp. 117 & 118—James lives in the peach stone house in Central Park. The Centipede becomes a VP of a boot/shoe company. The Earthworm is employed by a cosmetics firm. The Silkworm and Miss Spider set up a factory to make rope for tightrope walkers. The Glowworm lights the Statue of Liberty. The Grasshopper becomes a member of the New York Symphony Orchestra. The Ladybug marries the Head of the Fire Department.)

2. Which ending do you think is the most appropriate for the story character? Why? (Opinion—answers will vary. Discuss.)

Post-reading Activities

1. **Jingles** are poems that have obvious easy rhythm with a simple repetition of sounds. Jingles can be sung, chanted, or recited. Each jingle has a quality that remains in the minds of those hearing it. Create advertising jingles for the Centipede, (boot & shoes), Earthworm, (face cream), and the Silkworm and Miss Spider (rope). **For example:**

Centipede	**Earthworm**	**Silkworm & Spider**
Difficult to please?	*For Earthworm softness*	*For rope that's safe;*
Hard to fit?	*That is sheer delight,*	*For rope that's strong,*
Listen to the Centipede.	*Use our face cream*	*Use ours—by experts.*
Don't be in a snit!	*Morning, noon and night.*	*You can't go wrong.*

2.   Complete attribute webs.
3.   Complete story map.
4.   Write an epilogue about the life of James.

Conclusion

Discuss with the group, and relate to the story, one of the following proverbs or a proverb or poem of your own choice.

**There is nothing that cannot be
achieved by firm determination.
Japanese**

**To him who is determined it
remains only to act.
Italian**

**If friends have faith in each other, life
and death are of no consequence.
Chinese**

Supplementary Activities

Vocabulary Word Search Puzzle #1

Do the word search. Write down the letters that have not been used, starting at the top and working left to right in each row. Group letters into words to find out what kind of peach is growing on the old tree in the aunts' garden.

Words to Find

MAMMOTH

RIDICULOUS

SCARLET

CURIOUS

PADDLE

STAMPEDING

STONE

GAPE

MARVELOUS

HEAVE

VISIBLE

VENOMOUS

COMPLICATED

WITHERING

INTENTLY

FANTASTICALLYMI

RACULOUS

UPHILL

BOLT

TREMENDOUS

INSPECTING

DEPART

MARVEL

EXTRAORDINARY

M	A	M	M	O	T	H	P	V	T	I	I	D	T
A	I	C	G	I	S	E	A	E	R	N	E	E	F
R	V	R	U	A	X	A	D	N	E	S	T	P	A
V	B	I	A	R	P	V	D	O	M	P	W	A	N
E	R	O	S	C	I	E	L	M	E	E	I	R	T
L	A	O	L	I	U	O	E	O	N	C	T	T	A
O	R	D	I	T	B	L	U	U	D	T	H	N	S
U	P	H	I	L	L	L	O	S	O	I	E	S	T
S	C	A	R	L	E	T	E	U	U	N	R	T	I
R	I	D	I	C	U	L	O	U	S	G	I	O	C
C	O	M	P	L	I	C	A	T	E	D	N	N	A
A	R	S	T	A	M	P	E	D	I	N	G	E	L
I	N	T	E	N	T	L	Y	M	A	R	V	E	L
Y	E	X	T	R	A	O	R	D	I	N	A	R	Y

What kind of peach grows on the old tree in the garden?

__ __   __ __   __ __ __ __ __ __ __ __ __ __ __ __

Some other things to do:

1.   Put the words in alphabetical order.
2.   Number the words and:
     Define every odd-numbered word.
     Use every even-numbered word in a sentence.

Vocabulary Word Search Puzzle #2

Do the word search. Write down the letters that have not been used, starting at the top and working left to right in each row. Group letters into words to find out where James' adventure ends.

```
I N D E S T R U C T I B L E M A
N M O D E S T L Y T H V U N E N
T E B L U E B O T T L E R C L N
E P O E S C O R T E D R K A A O
R I I C U R R E N T T I S N U
R N L H O I S T E D I I N E C N
U N I T Y O L U N G E C G D H C
P A N F U N N E L S F A N E O E
T C G C H O R U S E D L R W L M
E L C L A M B E R E D L Y C Y E
D E L I C A T E L Y O Y R K H N
H O R I Z O N S T E A L T H Y T
P R O P O S A L T E E M I N G S
I N F E R I O R K A T Y D I D S
K I P P E R V I T A L F R O T H
```

Words to Find

INDESTRUCTIBLE
INTERRUPTED
VERTICALLY
HOISTED
FUNNELS
CLAMBERED
MELANCHOLY
HORIZON
STEALTHY
PROPOSAL
TEEMING
ANNOUNCEMENTS
KATYDIDS
IMBECILES
BLUEBOTTLE
MODESTLY
DELICATELY
LURKING
FROTH
KIPPER
VITAL
ENCASED
ESCORTED
CURRENT
CHORUSED
BOILING
PINNACLE
LUNGE
ARCH
INFERIOR

WHERE DOES THE ADVENTURE END?

___ ____ __

___ _____

Some other things to do:
1. Put the words in reverse alphabetical order, starting with VITAL and ending with ANNOUNCEMENTS.
2. Research **katydids** and **bluebottles**.

Vocabulary Crossword Puzzle #1

Match a vocabulary word, listed in "Vocabulary Words Used," with its definition, listed under "Across" or "Down." Fill in the puzzle using the correct vocabulary words.

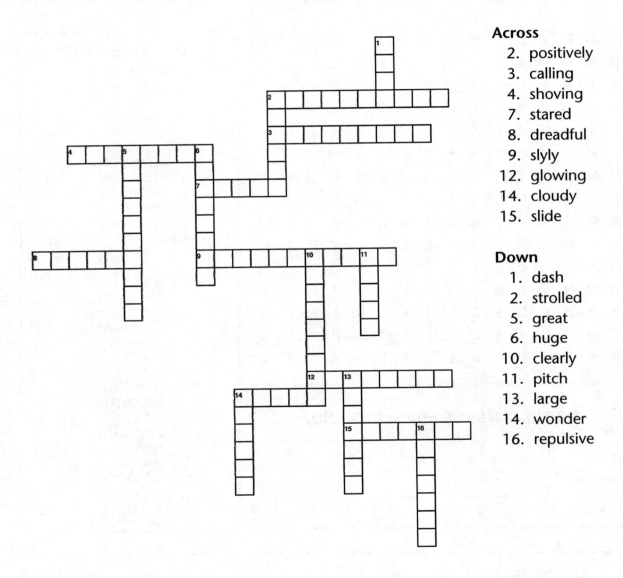

Across
2. positively
3. calling
4. shoving
7. stared
8. dreadful
9. slyly
12. glowing
14. cloudy
15. slide

Down
1. dash
2. strolled
5. great
6. huge
10. clearly
11. pitch
13. large
14. wonder
16. repulsive

Vocabulary Words Used: absolutely, ambled, beckoning, bolt, gaped, gigantic, hideous, horrid, insidiously, jostling, luminous, lurch, marvel, massive, murky, obviously, slither, tremendous

Vocabulary Crossword Puzzle #2

Match a vocabulary word, listed in "Vocabulary Words Used," with its definition, listed under "Across" or "Down." Fill in the puzzle using the correct vocabulary words.

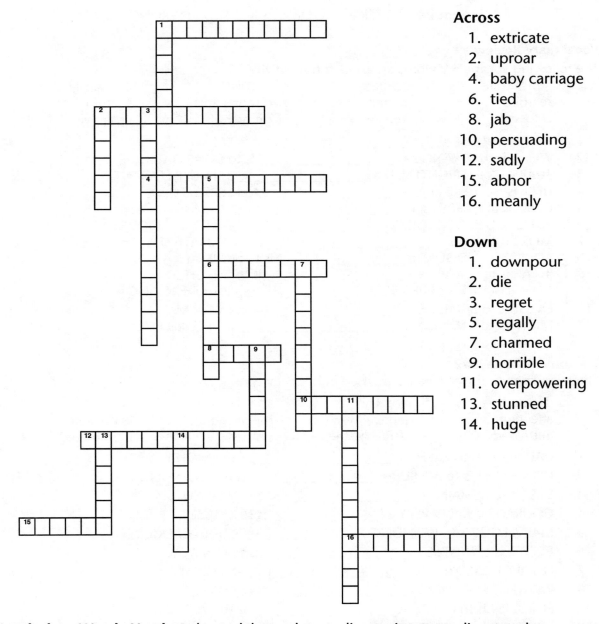

Across

1. extricate
2. uproar
4. baby carriage
6. tied
8. jab
10. persuading
12. sadly
15. abhor
16. meanly

Down

1. downpour
2. die
3. regret
5. regally
7. charmed
9. horrible
11. overpowering
13. stunned
14. huge

Vocabulary Words Used: aghast, deluge, detest, disappointment, disentangle, enthralled, exhorting, grisly, immense, lunge, majestically, malevolently, overwhelming, pandemonium, pathetically, perambulator, perish, tethered

Synonym or Antonym?

For each activity, match the synonym or antonym in the comparison with a listed vocabulary word.

Sample: BETTER is to WORSE as RIGHT is to WRONG.

Vocabulary Review #1
The following vocabulary words are used in this activity:

ramshackle	desolate	peculiar	cautiously
seething	magnificent	disagreeable	scornful
colossal	literally	ghastly	repulsive

1.   FIND is to LOSE as _____ is to PLEASANT.
2.   WEIRD is to STRANGE as _____ is to DILAPIDATED.
3.   SCARED is to FRIGHTENED as _____ is to UNPLEASANT.
4.   HERE is to THERE as _____ is to RESPECTFUL.
5.   GLAD is to HAPPY as _____ is to SPLENDID.
6.   FOOL is to BLOCKHEAD as _____ is to STUPENDOUS.
7.   MORE is to LESS as _____ is to FIGURATIVELY.
8.   ADMIRE is to DISLIKE as _____ is to NORMAL.
9.   BLEAK is to DREARY as _____ is to DESERTED.
10. COMPLIMENT is to PRAISE as _____ is to SHOCKING.
11. LARGE is to SMALL as _____ is to CALM.
12. MIRTH is to SADNESS as _____ is to CARELESSLY.

Vocabulary Review #2
The following vocabulary words are used in this activity:

destruction	serenely	chaos	vast
affectionately	frantically	menacing	loathsome
infuriated	flabbergasted	sinister	plummeted

1.   CAUTIOUS is to RASH as _____ is to COOLLY.
2.   CONFRONT is to AVOID as _____ is to ASCENDED.
3.   STAY is to REMAIN as _____ is to ENRAGED.
4.   COURAGE is to BRAVERY as _____ is to AMAZED.
5.   MARVELOUS is to WONDERFUL as _____ is to CALMLY.
6.   BETTER is to WORSE as _____ is to RENEWAL.
7.   FESTIVE is to JOYFUL as _____ is to IMMENSE.
8.   WRATH is to ANGER as _____ is to EVIL.
9.   FORLORN is to HAPPY as _____ is to HARMLESS.
10. SHOCKED is to HORRIFIED as _____ is to DISORDER.
11. LIMITED is to EXTENSIVE as _____ is to CALMLY.
12. ALIVE is to EXTINCT as _____ is to CHARMING.

1961

This book has a copyright date of 1961. In the story, the officers of the *Queen Mary* and the people of the City of New York are sure that the peach is a secret weapon or bomb of some kind. What was happening in the world at that time to cause such a reaction? Some examples follow:

- U.S. breaks off diplomatic relations with Cuba.
- Cuban exiled rebels attempt an unsuccessful invasion of Cuba at the Bay of Pigs; they were trained and supplied by U.S.
- Cuban leader Fidel Castro offers to trade 1,214 war prisoners for U.S. tractors.
- The practice of hijacking airplanes to Cuba is begun by Cuban nationals and Castro sympathizers.
- President Kennedy meets with Khrushchev in Vienna to discuss disarmament.
- The Berlin Wall is constructed in Germany.
- Spy trials take place in London.

The Place

In the story, when James has to go to live with his aunts, he misses the ocean very much. What place would you miss the most if you were not allowed to roam from your residence? (woods, prairie, desert, mountains, lake…) Describe the place and explain why you would miss it most of all.

Paper Dolls

On page 40, Aunt Sponge and Aunt Spiker are described as being as flat, thin and lifeless "as a couple of paper dolls." Make illustrations of the aunts as they might look as paper dolls—after they were run over by the peach.

Aunt Sponge   **Aunt Spiker**

Cloud-Men's City
The second full paragraph on page 100 describes some of the activities in the Cloud–Men's City. Create a large mural that depicts a Cloud–Men's City. Add materials to give the mural a three-dimensional effect (cotton, lace, netting, yarn, ribbon, glitter, etc.).

Recipe for "Cloud" Finger Paint
To one quart liquid laundry starch add enough soap flakes to obtain the desired consistency. Add tempera paint or food coloring. (About one teaspoon of tempera paint for each quart of the mixture is usually enough.) OR: Mix wheat paste with water to the desired consistency and add coloring.

Landmark Landing
Imagine that the giant peach landed on one of the following landmarks. Rewrite Chapters 38 and 39 to reflect your choice.

The Eiffel Tower	The Great Wall of China
The Leaning Tower of Pisa	A Different Landmark of Your Choice

A Special Friend
Imagine that you are friends with one of the travelers. Describe a special Saturday afternoon you spend together.

Ladybug	Miss Spider	Old Green Grasshopper
Earthworm	Centipede	Glowworm
Silkworm	James	

Teacher Information

Peach Tree
Botanists believe that the peach tree is native to China. From there, the fruit gradually spread westward. It is cultivated throughout warm temperate and subtropical regions of the world. Among the tree fruits, only the apple is more widely grown than the peach. Italy and the United States are the world's major peach-producing countries. There are nearly 300 varieties of peaches grown in the United States. The nectarine is a variety of peach.

Firefly
Fireflies, also called lightning bugs, are soft-bodied beetles and are found throughout tropical and temperate regions. Fireflies are named for the cold light emitted as a mating signal. They have luminescent glands located on the undersides of the rear abdominal segments. Each species has a unique signal. The luminescent larvae and wingless females of some species are called glowworms.

Ladybug

Ladybugs, or ladybird beetles, are found in temperate and tropical regions throughout the world. They are small, colorful beetles, having nearly circular bodies that are curved above and flat below. Although some ladybugs are unmarked, they are often red or orange above, with black, white, or yellow spots. Ladybugs are extremely beneficial for aphid and scale-insect control.

Centipede

Centipedes are arthropods with elongated, segmented, flattened, wormlike bodies with jointed appendages. Although the smaller centipedes are harmless to humans, the larger ones may have a poisonous bite that, in some species, is dangerous to humans. Centipedes are nocturnal and remain under stones or wood during the day. They are all carnivorous.

Silkworm

Silkworm is the common name applied to the silk-producing larvae of any of several species of moths. The best-known silkworm is the larvae of the common silkworm moth, *Bombyx mori*, which has been completely domesticated for the production of silk. Breeders have produced a variety that produces three broods of young annually. The silkworm caterpillars that are fed mulberry leaves produce the finest quality silk.

Spider

Spiders are carnivorous arthropods. They have eight walking legs, make extensive use of the silk that they spin, and most have poison glands associated with fangs on the anterior appendages. Spiders are numerous and worldwide. They are found on every continent except Antarctica. Spiders are able to live in almost every kind of terrestrial habitat. A few spiders have adapted to freshwater life by trapping air bubbles underwater and carrying the bubbles with them. Spiders are an important part of natural ecosystems because they primarily feed on other insects. The spider silk is used in the preparation of crosshairs in optical instruments, and spiders, themselves, are used to test certain drugs that may affect the building of webs.

Grasshopper

Grasshoppers are winged insects having hind legs that are specialized for jumping. They live on vegetation and are distributed worldwide wherever vegetation grows. Some grasshoppers are eaten and considered delicacies in many parts of the world. Only a few of the species of grasshoppers are pests. However, these can cause severe damage to field crops and pastures throughout the temperate and tropical zones.

Earthworm

Earthworms are segmented worms and play an important role in soil ecology. Soil is made more fertile by earthworms because their burrowing allows more air and water to reach deeper into the ground. Earthworms feed on decaying organic matter in the soil and deposit castings upon the ground which enriches the soil. Earthworms also are a source of food for many animals, and are the principal food of moles and shrews.

Empire State Building

Built in 1930-31, the Empire State Building in New York City was the tallest building in the world until 1971, when the first tower of the World Trade Center in that city was completed. Originally 1,250 feet height, The Empire State Building was increased to 1,472 feet with the addition of television antennas in 1950. Since it was opened during the depression, much of the building's rentable space remained vacant for a long time. The sightseers who paid to visit the observation decks actually paid the taxes levied on the building for several years. Built at a cost of 41 million dollars, the building was not structurally innovative. The large foyer and shimmering facade were the Empire State Building's most distinctive architectural characteristics designed by the firm of Shreve, Lamb and Harmon.

Bibliography

Dahl, Roald. *The BFG*. NY: Farrar, Straus, Giroux, 1982. **(Novel Units® guides available)**

Dahl, Roald. *Boy: Tales of Childhood*. NY: Farrar, Straus, Giroux, 1984.

Dahl, Roald. *Charlie and the Chocolate Factory*. NY: Viking Penguin, 1988, 1964. **(Novel Units® guides available)**

Dahl, Roald. *Charlie and the Great Glass Elevator*. NY: Knopf, 1972.

Dahl, Roald. *Danny, the Champion of the World*. NY: Bantam Books, 1978, 1975.

Dahl, Roald. *The Enormous Crocodile*. NY: Knopf, 1978.

Dahl, Roald. *George's Marvelous Medicine*. NY: Knopf, 1982, 1981.

Dahl, Roald. *Matilda*. NY: Viking Kestrel, 1988. **(Novel Units® guides available)**

Dahl, Roald. *The Twits*. NY: Knopf, 1981, 1980.

Dahl, Roald. *Rhyme Stew*. NY: Viking, 1990, 1989.

Dahl, Roald. *Roald Dahl's Revolting Recipes*. NY: Viking, 1994.

Dahl, Roald. *Roald Dahl's Revolting Rhymes*. NY: Bantam Books, 1986, 1982.

Allen, Missy. *Dangerous Natural Phenomena*. NY: Chelsea House, 1993.

Bailey, Jill. *The Life Cycle of a Grasshopper*. NY: Bookwright Press, 1990, 1989.

Bernhard, Emery. *Ladybug*. NY: Holiday House, 1992.

Bourgoing, Pascale de. *The Ladybug and Other Insects*. NY: Scholastic, 1991.

Branley, Franklyn. *It's Raining Cats and Dogs*. Boston, MA: Houghton Mifflin, 1987.

Catherall, Ed. *Exploring Weather*. Austin, TX: Steck-Vaughn, 1991.

Coldrey, Jennifer. *The Silkworm Story*. London: Deutsch, 1983.

Davies, Kay. *The Super Science Book of Weather*. NY: Thomson Learning, 1993.

Dorling Kindersley Vision. *See How Insects Grow*. (Video recording) NY: Sony Kids' Video, 1993. 1 videocassette, 30 minutes, VHS format.

Erlbach, Arlene. *Blizzards*. Chicago, IL: Children's Press, 1995

Fischer-Nagel, Heiderose. *Life of the Ladybug*. Minneapolis, MN: Carolrhoda, 1986.

Fradin, Dennis. *Blizzards and Winter Weather*. Chicago, IL: Childrens Press, 1983.

Glaser, Linda. *Wonderful Worms*. Brookfield, CT: Millbrook Press, 1992.

Godkin, Celia. *What About Ladybugs?* San Francisco, CA: Sierra Club Books for Children, 1995.

Greenbacker, Liz. *Bugs: Stingers, Suckers, Sweeties, Swingers*. NY: Watts, 1993.

Hawes, Judy. *Fireflies in the Night*. NY: HarperCollins, 1991.

Henwood, Chris. *Earthworms*. NY: Watts, 1988.

Hickman, Pamela. *Bugwise: Thirty Incredible Insect Investigations and Arachnid Activities.* Reading, MA: Addison-Wesley, 1991.

Jennings, Terry. *Earthworms.* NY: Gloucester Press, 1988.

Johnson, Sylvia. *Chirping Insects.* Minneapolis, MN: Lerner, 1986.

Johnson, Sylvia. *Fireflies.* Minneapolis, MN: Lerner, 1986.

Lampton, Christopher. *Blizzard.* Brookfield, CT: Millbrook, 1991.

McLaughlin, Molly. *Earthworms, Dirt, and Rotten Leaves: An Exploration in Ecology.* NY: Atheneum, 1986.

McVey, Vicki. *The Sierra Club Book of Weatherwisdom.* San Francisco, CA: Sierra Club Books, 1991.

Penny, Malcolm. *Discovering Spiders.* NY: Bookwright Press, 1986.

Preston-Mafham, Ken. *Discovering Centipedes and Millipedes.* NY: Bookwright Press, 1990.

Rogers, Daniel. *The Marshall Cavendish Science Project Book of Weather.* NY: Marshall Cavendish Corp., 1989.

Souza, Dorothy. *Eight Legs.* Minneapolis, MN: Carolrhoda Books, 1991.

Tannenbaum, Beulah. *Making and Using Your own Weather Station.* NY: Watts, 1989.

Watts, Barrie. *Ladybug.* Morristown, NJ: Silver Burdett, 1987.

Wechsler, Doug. *Bizarre Bugs.* NY: Cobblehill Books/Dutton, 1995.

Answer Key

Vocabulary Review #1: 1. repulsive; 2. ramshackle; 3. disagreeable; 4. scornful; 5. magnificent; 6. colossal; 7. literally; 8. peculiar; 9. desolate; 10. ghastly; 11. seething; 12. cautiously (Students may interchange answers 1, 3, and 10. You may wish to give them credit. Take the opportunity to discuss the shades of meaning of the similar words.)

Vocabulary Review #2: 1. affectionately; 2. plummeted; 3. infuriated; 4. flabbergasted; 5. serenely; 6. destruction; 7. vast; 8. sinister; 9. menacing; 10. chaos; 11. frantically; 12. loathsome (Students may interchange answers 8, 9, and 12. You may wish to give them credit. Take the opportunity to discuss the shades of meaning of the similar words.)

Word Search #1: IT IS EXTRAORDINARY

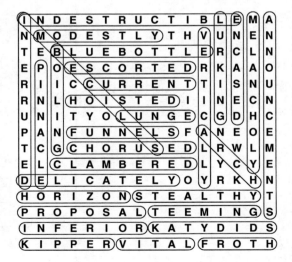

Word Search #2: THE CITY OF NEW YORK

CROSSWORD #1

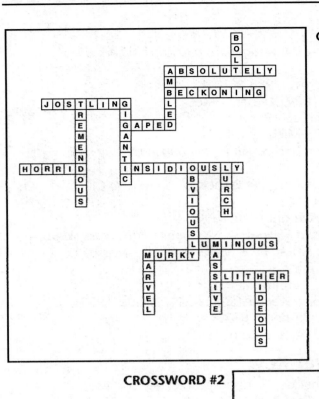

CROSSWORD #2

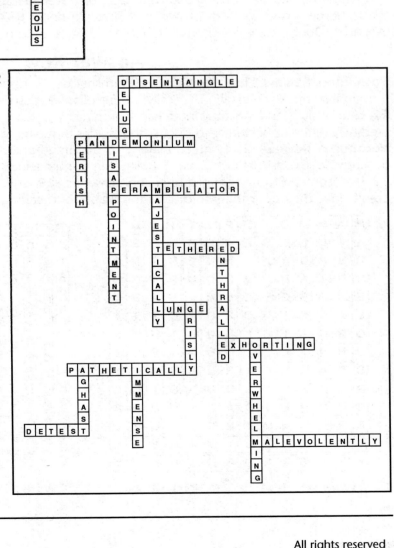

Vocabulary:

paddle: to move the hands or feet about in shallow water

ramshackle: dilapidated, shaky, decrepit, Ant.: substantial, solid

desolate: deserted, uninhabited, solitary, isolated; Ant.:inhabited, populated

peculiar: odd, strange; Ant.:normal, ordinary,

fantastically: grotesquely, eerily, marvelously; Ant.:mundanely, ordinarily

spectacles: eyeglasses

beckoning: calling, signaling

luminous: lustrous, brilliant, glowing, luminescent; Ant.: black, dull, cloudy, opaque

furiously: turbulently, wildly, fiercely; Ant.: tamely, blandly, weakly

centipedes: any of a class of long flattened many-segmented anthropoids with each segment bearing a pair of legs

hideous: repulsive, shocking, revolting; Ant.: attractive, charming

gracious: (good gracious)

ridiculous: ludicrous, senseless, foolish; Ant.: sensible, sound, serious

absolutely: perfectly, positively; Ant.: imperfectly, incompletely

extraordinary: unusual, amazing, remarkable; Ant.:ordinary, normal

mammoth: colossal, gigantic, huge; Ant.: dainty, petite, tiny

inspecting: examining, checking, studying

cautiously: warily, prudently, carefully; Ant.: rashly, carelessly

massive: large, imposing, impressive; Ant.: slight, delicate

marvel: wonder, phenomenon, curiosity; Ant.: normal, commonplace

shilling: former coin used in Great Britain, 1/20 of a pound

seething: boiling, raging, storming; Ant.: calm, subdued

miraculous: incredible, strange, wonderful; Ant.: usual, prosaic, ordinary

murky: misty, hazy, cloudy; Ant.: sunny, clear

curious: odd, strange, unique; Ant.: usual, ordinary

bittersweet: being at once bitter and sweet

uphill: ascending

gigantic: colossal, huge, enormous; Ant.: small, miniature, tiny

stone: the hard central portion of a fruit

bolt: rush, run, dash; Ant. walk, amble

reclining: lying back, sprawling, resting; Ant.: standing,

intently: attentively, raptly, earnestly; Ant.: carelessly, purposelessly

scarlet: bright red

magnificent: splendid, superb, lavish, elaborate; Ant.: modest, unostentatious

famished: starved; Ant.: full, sated

delicately: elegantly, nicely, deftly; Ant.: crudely, blatantly

positively: absolutely, undeniably, definitely; Ant.: possibly, perhaps, maybe

disagreeable: offensive, unpleasant, nasty; Ant.: genial, good-natured, amiable

marvelous: remarkable, exceptional, amazing; Ant.: commonplace
slither: glide, slink, slide, writhe
approval: act of approving[endorsing]
withering: devastating, cruel, crushing, murderous
scornful: contemptuous, disdainful, haughty; Ant.: respectful, approving, admiring
colossal: stupendous, vast, prodigious; Ant.: tiny, slight, miniature, Lilliputian
hysterics: a fit of uncontrollable laughing or crying
gossamer: something light, delicate— a film of cobwebs floating in the air in calm, clear weather
complicated: intricate, complex, involved; Ant.: plain, uniform,easy
ambled: strolled, sauntered, walked; Ant.: ran
literally: exactly, verbatim, actually; Ant.: figuratively, metaphorically
wretched: vile, despicable; Ant.: good, satisfactory, noble
heave: lift, rise, pitch, fling
obviously: clearly, plainly; Ant.: obscurely, indistinctly
depart: leave, go, withdraw; Ant.: remain, abide
ghastly: terrifying, shocking, terrible, grim; Ant.: inviting, pleasant
repulsive: repugnant, disgusting, obnoxious; Ant.: charming, pleasant
lurch: pitch, toss
venomous: deadly, malicious, cruel; Ant.: harmless, tolerant
insidiously: treacherously, slyly, stealthily; Ant.: openly, overtly
visible: observable, detectable; Ant.: imperceptible, hidden
horrid: repugnant, dreadful; Ant.: delightful, enchanting
gaped: stared, glared
panicked: became fearful
jostling: pushing, shoving,
hurtling: crashing, rushing, roaring
paddock: enclosure used for exercising animals
stampeding: retreating, fleeing, bolting
tremendous: great: Ant: small
destruction: havoc, ruin; Ant.: construction, renewal
serenely: calmly, tranquilly, peacefully; Ant.: turbulently,
indestructible: not destructible; Ant.: destructible
chaos: disorder, confusion, turmoil; Ant.: order, calm, tranquility
unfortunate: unlucky, ill-starred, doomed; Ant.: lucky, fortunate
disentangle: extricate
trifle: to some small degree
chorused: in unison
vertically: perpendicularly
vast: immense, extensive; Ant.: small, limited
bibbling: sipping, drinking

disappointment: regret, dissatisfaction; Ant.: satisfaction, happiness
perish: die, expire; Ant.: survive
grisly: horrible, frightful   ; Ant.: pleasant
affectionately: tenderly, fondly; Ant.: coolly, uncaringly
glorious: splendid, wonderful
anxiously: worriedly, nervously; Ant.: calmly, securely, indifferently
perambulator: baby carriage
lunge: jab, stab
aghast: stunned, horrified, dumbfounded
froth: bubbles, foam, lather
pandemonium: uproar, commotion, bedlam
pathetically: woefully, pitiably, sadly
exhorting: urging, persuading, spurring
frantically: agitatedly; Ant.: coolly, calmly
tethered: tied
majestically: nobly, regally, splendidly
clambered: climbed
spellbound: enthralled, fascinated
rambunctious: unruly, obstreperous; Ant.: tame, quiet
frantically: agitatedly; Ant.: stoically, calmly
menacing: threatening; Ant.: harmless
overwhelming: overpowering, stunning, devastating
loathsome: repulsive, disgusting; Ant.: charming, delightful
infuriated: enraged, angered; Ant.: appease, placate
enthralled: charmed, fascinated, beguiled
malevolently: evilly, hostilely, meanly; Ant.: kindly, friendly
flabbergasted: amazed, astonished; Ant.: unimpressed, unmoved
detest: abhor, loathe
immense: huge, massive, tremendous; Ant.: small, puny
deluge: flood, downpour, inundation
sinister: evil; Ant.: good
smithereens: fragments, bits
plummeted: plunged, dropped, fell; Ant.: ascend, rise
stupor: coma, faint, dullness

© Novel Units, Inc.

47

Definitions and Antonyms: Vocabulary Review #1

ramshackle: dilapidated, shaky, decrepit
desolate: deserted, uninhabited, solitary isolated
peculiar: odd, strange
cautiously: warily, prudently, carefully
seething: boiling, raging, storming
magnificent: splendid, superb, lavish, elaborate
disagreeable: offensive, unpleasant, nasty
scornful: contemptuous, disdainful, haughty
colossal: stupendous, vast, prodigious
literally: exactly, verbatim, actually
ghastly: terrifying, shocking, terrible, grim
repulsive: repugnant, disgusting, obnoxious

Antonyms
substantial, solid
inhabited, populated
normal, ordinary, common
rashly, carelessly
calm, subdued
modest, unostentatious
genial, good-natured, amiable
respectful, approving, admiring
tiny, slight, miniature, Lilliputian
figuratively, metaphorically
inviting, pleasant
charming, pleasant

Definitions and Antonyms: Vocabulary Review #2

destruction: havoc, ruin
serenely: calmly, tranquilly, peacefully
chaos: disorder, confusion, turmoil
vast: immense, extensive
affectionately: tenderly, fondly
frantically: agitatedly
menacing: threatening
loathsome: repulsive, disgusting
infuriated: enraged, angered
flabbergasted: amazed, astonished
sinister: evil
plummeted: plunged, dropped, fell

Antonyms
construction, renewal
turbulently
order, calm, tranquility
small, limited
coolly, uncaringly
stoically, calmly
harmless
charming delightful
appease, placate
unimpressed, unmoved
good
ascend, rise